Amazon FBA

Amazon FBA 2016 for Beginners

How To Make Money Online With Amazon and Create a Passive Income While You Sleep

by Donald Brown

I0492719

Table of Contents

Amazon FBA

Amazon FBA 2016 for Beginners

How To Make Money Online With Amazon and Create a Passive Income While You Sleep

Disclaimer

While all attempts have been made to verify the information provided in this book, the author does not assume any responsibility for errors, omissions, or contrary interpretations of the subject matter contained within. The information provided in this book is for educational and entertainment purposes only. The reader is responsible for his or her own actions and the author does not accept any responsibilities for any liabilities or damages, real or perceived, resulting from the use of this information.

Introduction

Amazon is one of the sites that have created a very advanced fulfillment network networks across the globe. It is this network that plays a central role in ensuring that your business benefits from the expertise it offers.

This is because it offers you as its client a place to store your products that you intend to sell. It then comes in to pick the products from storage, pack them and ship them to provide a customer-base for the products. Additionally, it is important to note that with Amazon, you can scale up your business and reach out to a wide range of clients across the globe.

With Fulfillment by Amazon (FBA), you as a client that wishes to sell your products has a fulfillment choice to market your products online. This is one of the best and easiest ways to make money as you sleep.

This is because; Amazon takes up the responsibility of selling its inventory in the market alongside your products. This means that when a product from a third party merchant is bought, the shipment of the product to the buyer is dependent on the fulfillment method that you selected as a seller of the product.

Additionally, merchants who make a choice to participate in FBA enjoy the packaging, sorting and shipment of the goods by Amazon. This is because there is ease in doing this by Amazon because it has over 13 warehouses in the United States that play a pivotal role in handling fulfillment.

This is for both Amazon as well as third party merchants. This means that Amazon goes the extra mile of helping those sellers that do not wish to bother with the process of fulfillment. Therefore, you can sell your products today on Amazon and enjoy your sleep as you get the money flowing into your account for every sale made.

It is important to note that sellers on Amazon often vary depending on the products that they wish to market through Amazon FBA, the margins, and category of the product as well as related merchant variables.

Chapter 1 - Why you should choose Amazon FBA

Fulfillment by Amazon is often preferred by a wide range of third-party merchants. This does not mean that it is right for the kind of business that you are doing. This means that it is necessary that you assess the major benefits that come along with faster shipping, easy returns as well as potentially attracting a wide clientele in comparison to the service fee incurred.

This is because sellers often take into consideration issues that we will discuss concerning sale tax compliance as well as commingling associated fraud. For some people, making a choice of selling through FBA or not is often a difficult decision.

However, I hope that you take into consideration using FBA and thus if you do, then it is important that you learn more about the integration of FBA more closely to another retail system that you participate in.

Fulfillment by Amazon is one of the best options for sellers who are looking for someone to ship their products while increasing the time of shipment and minimizing the cost that they have to incur in fulfillment. You therefore, have to realize that FBA offers a wide range of benefits that will earn you a lot of money while you enjoy your sleep. Some of these benefits include:

Discounted cost of shipment

Some of the most important factors that buyers consider while selecting the best fulfillment method to employ to purchase a product are the amount of time and the cost that they have to incur on a product.

With Amazon FBA, the products that you intend to sell are eligible to free shipment thus placing them at the top of the product list without having to incur any cost in the process.

Additionally, it is important to take into consideration the fact that prime members in FBA are offered a two-day free shipment on the items they sell through them. Additionally, for their customers, Amazon FBA customers often are eligible to free shipment especially if their orders exceed $ 35.

 When this happens to customers, others are attracted to buy more considering the incentive that the company offers.

Customer service and return management

With Amazon FBA, you are liable to acclaimed customer service as part of the process of fulfillment. This means that you can contact the customer support through your phone or email at any time of day or night.

This way, when you place your products on Amazon, you do not have to worry on frequent follow-ups because you now that your products are okay and thus instead, you can focus on management of other enterprise operations.

Additionally, choosing to sell and buy products on Amazon plays a crucial role in processing your returns through their fulfillment call center. This allows for convenient return items on a need basis and thus making it easy for you regarding the logistics that are involved in the process of returning the products.

However, it is important to note that there are charges that are involved in the return process for the service.

Multi-channel fulfillment

Most people often think that FBA is just for selling on Amazon. However, you can use Amazon FBA for your sales channels such as your website as well as other eCommerce platforms. In this manner, the clients can easily enjoy flexibility in shipping the products within a one-day, two-day as well as standard delivery turn-around times.

This often means that the process of handling fulfillment across a wide range of channels may be challenging and costly. However, Amazon plays a role in helping you handle this to ensure that the customers have the best experience possible.

This means that whether you are already selling on Amazon FBA or not, you have the ability to keep the ordering and shipment process at a high degree of consistency across your preferred channels.

Customer experience

Selling your products through Amazon FBA allows you as a merchant to reach to more customers through the enlarged customer base that the company has.

This allows you to attract a wide range of clientele through the services that FBA offers such as multiple options for shipment, fast delivery of products, easy return process as well as a customer service that you can trust.

This is often the case especially when customers see the Amazon FBA logo on your products. This is very useful in ensuring that you increase the number of sales and thus provide customer experience that ensures customer satisfaction.

Buy box share

Amazon FBA often impacts on the buy box share variables that include the rates of shipping and selling. This means that it plays a central role in boosting your probability of getting a share of the buy box for their products despite the challenges that are associated with eligibility requirements of the buy box.

Additionally, Amazon FBA offers branding services for their merchants. This is by carefully curating their brands to meet the needs of their customers thus making it easy for online shopping.

This means that FBA offers its customers a chance to align their stores with the brand and thus lending your store of products with a high reputation that attracts more clients into buying.

Chapter 2 - What is the cost of using Fulfillment by Amazon?

Once you have known the benefits that come along with using the Amazon FBA, it is important for you to understand its cost. This is pivotal in helping you in the process of determining the fitness of this service for your products and thus guiding you into making the right decision.

First, it is important to note that Amazon breaks down their costs based on the item type. The types of items include Media, non-media, oversize and the zero-fee fulfillment items.

This means that for the products that you are selling on this platform have the following costs: handling of orders per customer order, pick and pack per unit that is ordered by a customer, handling of the weight per pound per unit ordered as well as the storage per cubic foot on a monthly basis.

It is also important for you to bear in mind that there are products that have the additional fee applied to them. It is through certain scenarios that contribute to the price alteration from the standard pricing. Such scenarios include:

Items that are oversized and therefore require special ways of handling per shipment, inventories that are stored for more than six months, the time of the year often determines the storage fee charged as well as the cost per cubic foot on a monthly basis.

For instance, the price of storage often increases between October and December. Additionally, there are fee charges that are placed on processing customer returns on a specific line of products.

I want you to think about your business for a second, what are some of the products that you sell? If you are selling oversized products, inventories that have long shelf lives or desire to use the FBA just for the holiday season, then it is important to note that you are subject to incurring additional costs.

Based on the fact that businesses often deal with different types of products, Amazon FBA offers a revenue calculator that calculates the cost and the possible revenue of using their services.

This tool is a great one especially if you intend to sell a few products to make a comparison of the fact that you are already selling on Amazon. You can use this tool to check what products will sell with a high level of profits

Disadvantages of Amazon FBA

In spite the fact that Amazon FBA remains the best fulfillment service across the globe, It is important to note that there are a few demerits that often go without the realization of most merchants as well as buyers.

 This means that when you are starting off business with this company, it is important that you are aware of these demerits that may be associated with the services.

Commingling merchandise

With the Amazon FBA company, there is a shipment of products from a wide range of facilities across the nations thus ensuring that the products reach the buyers at a very short turn-around time.

This is the reason the services that are offered are quite efficient. To ensure the same efficiency to the merchants that sell their fulfilling products through FBA, the option of commingling is given.

This means that there is a combination of the qualifying products from wide range of sellers for them to be processed and shipped by FBA. This means that as a seller, it saves you time and the strain that you might have otherwise spent applying for approved labels for each of your items or making payments to Amazon to do it for you.

This means that instead of providing labels, you can easily use an item barcode that pools your products with other sellers by the identification (ID) of the product. This way, Amazon can store the products strategically and ship them using the same product ID by location that ensures that the products reach the customers very fast. So what is the problem?

The quality control of the product often is a challenge for the sellers. There are quite some scenarios that have happened where the sellers are forced to close shops, get negative reviews or even worse, and face legal actions when their products are counterfeited or are damaged before they can reach the hands of the customers despite the genuine products that the sellers sent to Amazon.

You have to realize that this is not the fault of the seller despite the fact that they have to face harsh consequences.

Sale tax compliance

Another issue that has been voiced after the use of Amazon FBA for selling products is that related to issues of sale tax compliance.

This often is the case because Amazon does not tell the sellers which one of their warehouses houses their products. Additionally, they do not provide the sellers with a list of warehouses where items are located.

This means that sellers are not quite certain where they should register for sale tax compliance. This is because they do not know the location or the products and the customers until the transaction is complete.

This means that the sellers are put at a risk of exposure to liability issues. Along with the high cost that is associated with this process, you have to take into consideration a wide range of factors before taking the step of doing business on Amazon FBA.

Mostly, the products that you have often influence the individual product margins, thus, limiting profits. However, you have to bear in mind that the increase in the total sales, as well as the exposure of your products, offers a great investment option for your online store.

This means that whenever you have less money for a particular product that you are selling, you may sell them on Amazon FBA and have overall huge profits on the products sold. You have to remember that you are not being forced into selling your products on FBA, and thus you can take the time that you need to calculate whether you are likely to make profits.

Chapter 3 - How to use Amazon FBA to Make Money

When considering using FBA for your products, you have to remember that it is quite easy and efficient for both you and your customers. There are quite some steps that you have to follow when beginning to use Amazon FBA. These steps include:

Step 1: Send your products to Amazon

The first step is by first uploading your listings to the seller central on Amazon FBA and then allows them to fulfill all or part of your products. Then print the PDF labels that are will be provided to you by Amazon using the FBA label services.

Then proceed to use Amazon discounted shipment services or make a choice of the appropriate carrier for the delivery of your products.

Step 2: Amazon FBA product storage

The second step is the storage of your products by Amazon FBA warehouse. This is usually in a ready-to-ship inventory. Therefore, it is the work of FBA to receive and scan your inventory of the products listed.

They then record the unit dimensional measurements of the products for storage. You then have to monitor the inventory of your products using an integrated tracking system at the Amazon FBA.

Step 3: Ordering of the products by the customers

At this stage, the most important thing that you have to bear in mind is that Amazon FBA fulfills all the orders that are made on sales, not on Amazon or those that are placed directly on Amazon.com.

The listings of your products that are intended for selling are often listed in the hierarchy of their prices without any shipping costs. This is because they qualify for free shipment especially in cases of eligible orders.

Additionally, the prime members at Amazon often are offered an opportunity of upgrading their shipment options for the eligibility in the FBA listings. This step often excludes multi-channel fulfillment orders from other sites and services that include the web stores in Amazon and the Amazon checkouts.

Step 4: Amazon picks and pack products

In this step, it is the role of the Amazon FBA services to ensure that they have picked the products that are detailed in the inventory and then packs them before they are delivered to the customers that ordered them.

This is by ensuring that they locate the products using their advanced warehouses through the web. This is then followed by picking of the products at a very high speed and then sorted through the system. The customers have the ability to combine the products with others that are fulfilled by Amazon.

Step 6: Shipment of your products by Amazon

It is this step that involves the shipment of the products to the customers from the Amazon FBA centers. The shipment method that is utilized by the Amazon FBA is dependent on the choice that the customer has requested.

 Additionally, the Amazon FBA often offers information tracking services for their customers. However, in the case of the orders that are present on Amazon.com, Customers have the freewill to contact the customer service concerning the same.

Step 1: Getting started on Amazon FBA

For you to get started on Amazon by adding fulfillment by Amazon to your selling account, you first begin by clicking on the inventory Icon on Amazon website. Ten make a selection of Manage inventory.

Then select the product that you wish to include as an FBA listing. This is achieved by checking the box that is adjacent to it on the far left of the column. Then from the pull-down menu on the actions icon, select change to "fulfilled by Amazon" Then on the next page that appears, select the convert button and then keenly follow the instructions that are provided on creating you first shipment.

How then can you make money through Fulfillment by Amazon?

There are quite some tips that are very important in contributing to you taking advantage of the services that are offered by Amazon for the advantage of your business.

Some of these tips include:

Pull all your expenses on your reward credit cards

Aside from the inventory of the listings of products that you are marketing through Amazon FBA, ensure that all these are on your credit cards. This is very important in ensuring that you accumulate the best possible ROI.

Select a niche

Ensure that when you are selling on Amazon FBA, you can stick to a single line of products. It is this way that you can be able to tell what products sell well and what products do not sell well. This way, you will be able to make the right decision on whether it is worth selling there or not based on the amounts of profits that you get.

Also, you can choose to sell items that have a lower selling fee that is applied to them in order to incur the least amount of cost but still accumulate many profits. The most important decision that you have to make is targeting physical products focused niches as well as the use of keywords.

This is because it is easy to make money through the FBA Amazon affiliate program especially in cases where people are coming to the site to look for a specific product that is discussed or offered by your website. You have to note that it is challenging to use blogs to make money. This is because when they come there, they are looking for advice and not the product itself.

Price the items that you intend to sell

According to people that have used Amazon FBA for an extended period, there is evidence that pricing the products that you are selling allow you to sell these goods within the shortest time possible.

This is because those good at appearing at the top of the product listing often get the attention of the potential buyers and thus selling much faster compared to those that do not feature anywhere in the price listing.

Plan appropriately for returned or damaged good

Once you have made shipment of your box off to Amazon FBA, you have to realize that you are not in control of the product anymore. This means that what happens to the product along the shipment routes is not in your control, but if anything happens to it, then you are responsible for them.

 However, Amazon's 100 % satisfaction guarantee often spills over to the probable buyers of your products. This means that as you take into consideration pricing of your items, it is important to factor in approximately 3-5 % of the items that are put up for sale to come back due to damage or other factors and fail to resell again.

Use product images clickable affiliate links

According to one of the merchants that has made huge amounts of money through the FBA center on Amazon, it is evident that using products images in making sales often attracts a wide range of clientele.

This way, the interest of the customers is geared on what the product can do and because of the satisfaction that they get from viewing the product, they then buy more. Over 15% of the products that Chris sold on Amazon had product images clickable affiliate links on them.

Chapter 4 - Reasons why FBA is a triple win!

There are quite some factors that you have to realize about FBA that makes it a triple win and are the main reasons why you have to use this service. These factors include:

Higher prices, higher margins as well as higher payouts

Since the products were sold through FBA, they are often eligible for Free Super Saver shipment as well as Amazon Prime services. This is because when you sell your items through Amazon FBA, you can raise the prices to coincide with those of your competitors' total prices.

This means that you set the prices of your products to be equal to the sum of their prices and the shipment cost. This way, once the FBA fee is factored in, you still receive a high net payout from the Amazon sale of your products based on the high sale price. For instance, a seller selling their products at $30 and a shipment cost of $5 will be quite similar to you selling on FBA at a price of $35.

This makes you as an FBA seller a tie breaker!

Less work

One of the most important things that you have to bear in mind is the fact that selling using the Fulfillment by Amazon services allows you to sell your products 24 hours a day for seven days a week. This means that the process of shipping the products to the clients is done throughout the week as well as during the weekends.

Additionally, the shipment of the products can take place when the seller is at home or on vacation. This is the case because once you have prepared the products for the warehouse and send them to Amazon; you do not have to do anything else. All you have to do is to monitor the inventory of your products and make adjustments to the prices as required remotely from where you are.

You do not have to keep a stock of your products in boxes or envelopes among other packaging materials or shipment labels anymore. Additionally, you do not have to keep going to the post-office each day to check for deliveries.

Happy clients

According to research, it is estimated that over half of the customers who buy from Amazon have not used a third party merchant before. This is because Amazon customers often wish to purchase their products from other one-on-one business enterprises.

However, their trust for Amazon has grown tremendously based on the fact that the products that they have ordered through FBA will take the shortest time possible to be shipped to them.

Additionally, clients have the certainty that of there is a problem that arises during the process of shipment such as extended return policy; Amazon will help.

You have to bear in mind that when your products are shipped through Amazon FBA services, they often attract a wide range of clientele who are willing to pay more for their products to be shipped through Amazon.

This is one of the most important points that you have to keep with you as you take a step to making money with Amazon FBA. Amazon buyers are willing to pay more money just so that their products come from Amazon FBA sellers. The reason why they do this is that they trust the FBA services based on the fact that they are top-notch regarding quality and delivery services.

Scalability

With the introduction of Fulfillment by Amazon services, the competitive advantage that most sellers out there often enjoyed exists no more. This means that sellers at the Amazon FBA often are at a position of making more money by selling items that they have online.

This is based on the fact that initially, they had a lot of products that they did not have enough space for storage and they did not also have the time to sell them due to other commitments.

With Amazon FBA services, they can manage a large inventory of products. This is because; Amazon takes care of their concerns which are mainly space limitation and time.

Remember that, if you are a small seller, you do not have enough space for storage of your products. Additionally, you may not have all the time that is required to make sales, list the products as well as ship the products to the buyers that have ordered them. This is because, at first, you may think that ten orders are fun, twenty orders exciting but as they keep increasing per day to over 400 orders, what will you do?

Will you be able to manage? What happens when you go on vacation? The most probable answer, in this case, is that you may have to shut down the business for a while.

Now, Fulfillment by Amazon offers you an opportunity to sell your products and scale up your business without having to worry about time or even vacation. Additionally, if the business is making more sales a day, FBA can take care of that! This then allows you to compete with larger business on the same level.

This means that your ability to scale up the business is not restricted whatsoever. So what are you waiting for? If you have products to sell through FBA, sign up today and sell your products and make lots of money while you sleep. You can sell up to 500 products a day or even more than that in a week.

Manage your inventory in a wise way and you could run a Fulfillment by Amazon Empire from your bed!

Conclusion

It is evident from the literature and practical experience that I have had with Fulfillment with Amazon that it is an innovative service. This is no question of the quality of service that the clients using this service get for selling their products through this platform.

This is because as a seller; all you have to do is send your inventory directly to Amazon for storage. You have the ability to securely manage the inventory from a cloud-controlled facility.

Once the orders are received, it is the responsibility of Amazon to pick the products from their warehouse storage, pack them appropriately and ship them to their clients directly.

Additionally, it is important to note that Fulfillment by Amazon has the capacity and the expertise to process over a million of orders annually while maintaining their high reputation as one of the most trusted service providers across the globe.

This is because their services are of high quality while ensuring that they keep customer-satisfaction a priority hence ranking the highest among the e-commerce companies on the international front. The fact that they can maintain an advanced online order processing capacity as well as fulfillment operations across the world is amazing.

The fact that the company employs an advanced web-to-warehouse services in addition to the high speed at which they process their orders and deliver them to the customers makes it one of the top-notch priorities that you can take advantage of.

In addition to all the merits that we have discussed, Amazon FBA employs the use of a sophisticated sorting system that ensures that there is a complete shipment of the products to their clients. It is with the help of this technology that clients can get what they ordered whenever they place an order through the platform.

Whether your intention is to sell a few items and ship them weekly or millions of items and orders annually, you can take advantage of the expertise and the experience that Amazon has to offer your business through Fulfillment by Amazon!